Competition

Deal with it

from start to finish

Mireille Messier • Illustrated by Steven Murray

James Lorimer & Company Ltd., Publishers
Toronto

Today's the day!

It's the big game, and you are playing in it. Everyone will be there, and all eyes will be on you.

Just the thought of it has you sweating bullets. You've had a hard time sleeping for a couple of days and now your stomach is feeling queasy and nauseous.

Competition has given you a bad case of the jitters.

Everyone gets nervous before a competition. But we all react differently to the situation. Some people feel confident, and others get stressed. Some get energized, while others become aggressive. Some feel sick about it, and others try to avoid it all together. The drive to win and the fear of losing can sometimes make us do some pretty crazy stuff. When competition goes bad, it can get ugly — cheating, name calling, and bad sportsmanship are things we can all do without.

Competition is all around us.

We encounter it at school, at home, with friends, as well as during sports and other activities. It's impossible to completely avoid competition in everyday life. Luckily, there are ways of handling competition that can make it manageable and even fun.

This book will help you to understand what competition is, how to deal with it in a healthy way, and what to do when competition takes a nasty turn.

Contents

Everyone wants to be the best, right? ...

having fun

cooperating with your teammates

It doesn't take a brain surgeon to know what competition is: it's when a person or a group tries to be the best at something. What isn't so clear is when competition is healthy, and when it isn't. Competition can lead to good things, like...

studying hard for an upcoming test

being happy but humble about success

practicing your technique at a sport

playing by the rules

congratulating the winners after a game

But when the fear of losing comes into play, it might make you do negative things, like...

forfeiting a game when it looks like you're losing

cheating in order to win or get a better grade

bragging when you do well

accusing the winners of cheating or the referee of being biased

always trying to "one-up" friends with the latest gadget or gizmo

not letting teammates have their turn

doing things that are dangerous to your health to get an edge over the competition or to impress others

losing your temper and verbally or physically attacking someone

We've all won and we've all lost. It's part of life. The important thing is to know how to do both gracefully... even if it's not always easy!

LOSER

Competition can make

CHEATER

WINNER

TEAMMATE

you a *poor* . . .

Competition 101

QUIZ

When it come to winning or losing, most of us would much rather win. That's just human nature! Unfortunately, losing is often part of the game. In the following situations, are the kids reacting in a positive or negative way to the pressures of competition? Check out the answers on the opposite page.

3 The referee gives Max a penalty for obstruction. Max swears at the referee and tries to pick a fight.

1 Every time Linda plays Monopoly with Colin and Amanda she changes the rules to make things go her way. Her friends now refuse to play with her.

4 Joey is thinking about taking steroids to help him bulk up. He is certain it will give him the edge he needs for a popular girl to notice him.

2 Before every soccer game, Luke spends a few minutes imagining himself playing well.

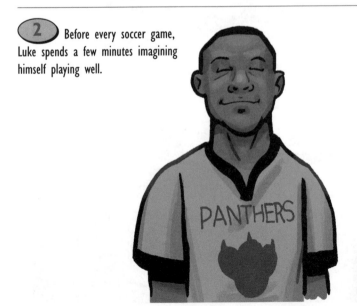

5 Alexa and Lynn are identical twins who constantly argue over stuff like "who got what," and "who's Mom's favourite."

6 Every time Tamara gets an A+ she rubs it in people's faces. This is really getting to her friends, and lately they've been avoiding her.

7 Laura is designated team leader for a project worth 40% of the class grade. She makes sure that everybody on her team has something fun and important to do.

8 Rostam has been unbeatable at "Conquest of the Valley." Kevin has rigged the LAN-party so that only he will be able to use the cheat codes. His victory is now assured!

9 Ian has a nasty habit of yelling distracting and obscene things at opposing team members every time they are up for a penalty shot to make them fumble and miss.

10 Christine is serious about getting into an elite university. She studies hard and often passes up going out with friends so that she can cram for an upcoming test.

Answers

1. Negative. Nobody wants to play with someone who can't lose. Linda's need to win is costing her friends.

2. Positive. This technique is called visualization. It helps you relax and focus before a big game or a test by thinking encouraging thoughts.

3. Negative. Part of good sportsmanship is accepting rulings, no matter how upset you are. Max could be penalized for his behaviour.

4. Negative. Taking any kind of substance to increase your performance or size is dangerous. Joey's health is way more important than who he dates.

5. Negative. When brothers and sisters compete for things or for attention it's called sibling rivalry. In this case, the siblings are overly competitive.

6. Negative. The only thing worse than a sore loser is a sore winner. Gloating is a sure-fire way to lose friends. Modesty is key when you win.

7. Positive. It can be hard to delegate work to others when a good grade is riding on the whole team's performance. Laura is showing trust and good leadership qualities.

8. Negative. As frustrating as constantly losing can be, stacking the game so that you have an unfair advantage is cheating.

9. Negative. Purposely disturbing the opponent is disruptive and rude. Ian's behaviour is a form of cheating and shows that he is a sore loser.

10. Positive. Christine knows what her goal is and has chosen to work hard to achieve it, no matter how tough it is at times.

Dear Competition Counse

Q.•At exam time I get very nervous. My stomach is in knots and I have a hard time •sleeping. Why does this happen to me? I'm usually so mellow.   — *Tossin' 'n' Turnin'*

A.•It's normal to be a little nervous before exams. Some people put a lot of pressure on •themselves (and sometimes on others) to do well in school. This can lead to sleeplessness, irritability, nail biting, and other symptoms of anxiety. A good way to manage tension is to study properly, eat and sleep well, and visualize yourself doing well during the exam. If you are still feeling uncontrollably nervous at exam time, you may want to discuss this with a guidance counsellor, teacher, or parent.

Q: **When I go to my school's hockey games, I've noticed that it's the adults who do a lot of the name-calling and screaming at the referee. Sometimes it gets so bad that I feel embarrassed to be seen near them! Is this normal?** — *Rinked Off*

A: You're reaction is completely normal. Competitiveness is not something that only affects kids – adults can also be poor sports. I suggest you mention your concern to the coach or another adult. He or she may be able to ask the adults to refrain from this kind of behaviour without singling you out. After all, you're probably not the only one who feels this way.

Q: **Since grade school my best friend and I have been trying really hard to get good grades. If she has 88% in French class, I'll try even harder to get a 95% or even 100% on the next test. Is this OK?** — *Striving for Perfection*

A: What you are experiencing is positive peer pressure, and it's great! Some people react very well to competition — it pumps them up and gives them that extra push to do better. As long as you and your friend are happy competing with each other, and it's all done in good fun, this is a healthy kind of competition.

Q: **I play cards with my six-year-old cousin, and he can get really upset when he loses too often. Is it all right to change the rules of a game to let him win sometimes ?** — *Ruled Out*

A: A game is more fun when both teams are of equal strength. When you play against a younger player you obviously have the upper hand. To even out the odds, it's okay to play with a handicap; for example, you could play with fewer cards, or he could have two turns for every one of yours. This way you've levelled the playing field while still having fun.

Q: **My best friend is boring. She refuses to play games that have winners and losers. She only wants to play "cooperative games" where "everybody wins." How can I get her to stop being such a wuss?** — *I Wanna Win*

A: If win/lose games are not your friend's bag, then you should respect that. There's a lot to be said for cooperative games. They teach you to work as a team in order to reach a common goal — something that is very valuable in everyday life. Also, is it possible that your friend doesn't want to play competitive games with you because of how you react to competition? Think about how you act when you win or lose and consider whether this may be the reason she doesn't want to compete with you.

Myths

All you need to be a winner is a **winning attitude.**

A positive attitude will help you compete successfully, but losing will always be part of the game. If you think you can simply "decide" to become a winner, you're bound to be disappointed sometimes.

If you **want something bad enough,** it will happen.

Wanting something bad enough to make yourself sick, to cheat, or become sad is unhealthy and it can result in tunnel vision — a state in which nothing but the win matters. Try to keep things in perspective.

Oh, good.
I lost.

Losing builds character.

Too much losing feels terrible and can affect the way you approach competition. If constantly losing is making you miserable, try your hand at something else.

- Children first play alone, then alongside others. By age 5, we have learned to play with — and against — others.

It's a dog-eat-dog world.

It's not only the aggressive, cutthroat competitors who get anywhere. Friendly competition and cooperation can lead to a wonderful job and an exciting life.

The point of competition is to win.

Well, one of the points of competition is to win. But if that's the only reason you compete at something, then you've missed the point.

All's fair in love and war.

This popular expression would have you believe that cheating is all right in certain circumstances. It never is!

- In "cooperative games" the whole team shares a goal and everyone wins or loses together.

- Research shows that "cooperative games" lead to improved social skills, self-confidence, and more optimistic attitudes.

What's wrong with being the best?

Doesn't everyone like winning and hate losing? All right, so you like to rub a victory in the loser's face. And maybe you only do stuff when you know you're going to come out on top. And, okay, sometimes you might cheat a little to make sure things end up the way they should. That doesn't mean you're overly competitive.

Does it?

DEAR DR. SHRINK-WRAPPED...

Q. **What's the deal? My folks keep going on and on about how the important thing in competition is to do your best and all that jazz. But then they turn around and build a shrine for all my brother's trophies. They go gaga when he wins! What gives? Is winning important or not?**
— *Confused about Competing*

A. Dr. Shrink-Wrapped knows that teachers and parents often send out mixed messages about competition. They say that winning is not the most important thing, but they also go over the top in praising the winners. The media does that same thing — how many interviews have you seen with the losing team or the third runner-up, compared to the time that is given to the winners?

Most people understand that winning is not the be-all and end-all. We like to think we are above such pettiness, and so we repeat what we know is right: the important thing is not winning, but how you play the game.

If you've ever won anything (which of course, you have!) you know what a rush it can be. The positive charge of winning is something that everyone would love to hold on to and be a part of. Unfortunately, it is also why people often put aside all of their wisdom about competition and give in to their need to be a star, or be connected to one.

Dr. Shrink-Wrapped suggests that you mention to your parents the mixed messages they are sending you. They probably have not noticed that they are doing this, and would be more careful if they knew how it is affecting you.

The Competitor

QUIZ

Sore loser. Cocky winner.

Remind you of anyone? Answer the following true or false questions to find out where you weigh in on the competition scale.

1. I've lost my temper at a call made by a referee.

2. I've cheated on tests.

3. I've copied homework off of others and passed it off as my own.

4. Some people refuse to play against me.

5. I don't care whose feelings I hurt as long as I win.

6. I have a reputation for being a tough competitor.

7. I often call people losers.

8. I've plagiarized information from books or Web sites.

9. I've mouthed off at people who did better than I did.

10. I've refused to shake the winner's hand.

11. I've refused to work with a weaker student on a team project.

12. I don't trust my teammates to do their jobs.

13. I know I'm the best one on my team.

I often take up challenges simply to prevent others from winning. **14**

I have plotted against someone to make them lose. **15**

I sometimes quit a game if it looks as though I could lose. **16**

I change the rules in my favour during games. **17**

I've used computer cheat codes while playing against unsuspecting competitors. **18**

I refuse to play against strong competitors. **19**

I've broken or thrown things in anger after a loss or a bad call. **20**

I've purposely tried to injure other players. **21**

I go out of my way to rub my success in the loser's face. **22**

I've accused people of cheating to make my loss seem unfair. **23**

I would never be seen with someone who is not from my clique. **24**

I've spread rumours about my opponents. **25**

When in the stands, I shout insulting things at the opposing team. **26**

I think that weak players should quit the game. **27**

I feel that only winners get anywhere in life. **28**

I know it's okay to bend the rules. **29**

I would rather forfeit the game than lose. **30**

Did you score a lot of Trues? You likely have an unhealthy attitude toward competition. Maybe it's time to talk to someone about how to have fun again when you compete.

The **Competitor**

Winning Ways

If you are the type of person who gets very aggressive — even hot-tempered — when competition is involved, here are some ways you can keep your outbursts in check (and keep your friends, too!).

Be a Sport

After a lost game or a low grade, it's sometimes hard to accept defeat. Your instinct might be to act out in anger. This behaviour is okay in very young children who don't understand how to handle the pressures of losing but, as you get older, flare-ups are not cool! Being a good sport — someone people enjoy playing with

and competing against — takes maturity. If you can walk away from a loss gracefully, everyone wins. Here are things you can you do to be a good sport:
• congratulate the winner.
• learn from your mistakes.
• strive to be better next time.
• be humble about your triumphs.

Cooperate

Aggressive competitors tend to have a hard time cooperating with others. How many times have you refused to pass the ball or share work with others in your group in order to keep control of the outcome? While trying so desperately to win — games or grades — you've also managed to upset all the people around you. If you have a hard time letting others do their share because you can't bear to lose, here are a few tips:
• Be patient: keep in mind that the only way your teammates will get better is by letting them do their share.
• Farm out: by delegating, you show respect and trust in others.
• Share: when

you try to do everything yourself, your chance of succeeding is diminished.
• Be a team player: a win is much more gratifying and a loss is easier to handle when everyone on the team did their best.

Play Fair

Tempted to cheat? Who wouldn't be? You get to win without having to do the hard work, the practicing, the studying — whatever. But if everybody cheated, what would be the point of competition? Fair play is an essential part of competition. If you are tempted to cheat, plagiarize, or lie, keep this in mind:
• Once you have a reputation as a cheater it's very hard to change it, no matter how you behave afterwards.
• Getting caught for cheating is much worse than a bad grade or losing a game. You could flunk,

DID YOU KNOW ?

• Arguments can turn into fights when people would rather

"win" than understand one another's viewpoints.

get benched, or even be expelled.
• A day will come when you won't be able to cheat, and your lack of real talent will be exposed.
• Cheating, even when you don't get caught, has an effect on your self-esteem, your friendships, and your ability to be proud of what you can achieve.

Keep Perspective

When winning becomes your only reason for competing, things can — and often do — go wrong. If you are so focused on the win that nothing else matters — including others' feelings, fair play, cooperation, and having fun — then you need to remember this:
• You will still be the same person whether you win or lose.
• Losing is disappointing, but it's not a matter of life and death.
• Why are you competing? Are your reasons healthy ones? If not, rethink whether you should be competing at all.
• Sometimes losing can actually open a door that you never would have considered otherwise.

✓ Do acknowledge the winner's accomplishments when you lose.

✓ Do accept praise kindly when you win.

✓ Do practice your skills and techniques to be at your best.

✓ Do welcome others' comments and advice with an open ear.

✓ Do stay cool under pressure.

✓ Do allow others to help you and trust them to do their share.

✓ Do respect the rules of the game.

✓ Do have a positive attitude.

✗ Don't cheat.

✗ Don't insult the winner.

✗ Don't accuse others of cheating.

✗ Don't compete only for the sake of winning.

✗ Don't rub it in when you win.

• Students who fear competition often fear other forms of conflict, such as confrontations and arguments.
• Competition is more enjoyable when participants feel they have an equal chance of succeeding.

The **Underdog**

Would you rather fake being sick or show up late than play a sport or take an exam? Have you ever heard adults or teachers refer to you as an "underachiever" or say that

"you are not living up to your potential."

If the answer is yes, you are not alone.
Sometimes it's hard for parents and teachers not to cross the line between encouraging you to do your best and pressuring you to be the

best. But most people face some kind of competition every day. If your reaction is to avoid competition like the plague, you will be cheating yourself out of some good opportunities to get to know people — including yourself — and maybe to have some fun doing it.

do's and don'ts

✓ Do prepare for upcoming events.

✓ Do try to relax and imagine yourself succeeding.

✓ Do have a Plan B in case something doesn't pan out.

✓ Do have a positive and enthusiastic approach to competition.

✗ Don't put all your eggs in one basket.

✗ Don't invent "doomsday" scenarios where everything goes wrong.

✗ Don't pretend you are above competition and put down the efforts of others.

✗ Don't put off practicing or studying for important events.

✗ Don't bottle up your feelings about the negative pressures that others may be putting on you to succeed.

✓ Do try different activities to see which is most suited to your tastes and talents.

✓ Do be realistic about your goals.

✓ Do let people know if they are putting too much pressure on you to succeed.

✗ Don't panic when you can't understand part of a test.

✗ Don't avoid competition out of fear of losing your friends' approval.

✗ Don't invent excuses for not competing.

The **Underdog**

QUIZ

Game On!

When the chips are down, there are basically three ways you can choose to react to competition. Ideally, you take up the challenge with enthusiasm and do your best (Game on). You could become too aggressive in your quest to win (Foul). Or you can decide to steer clear of it entirely to avoid losing (No show). Take this quiz and then check on the opposite page to see if your response to competition is a **FOUL**, **NO SHOW**, or **GAME ON**!

HESITANT PRESIDENT

1 Your friend has nominated you to run for class president. Do you: a) Say yes, and start working on your campaign? b) Say yes, and start spreading rumours about the other two candidates? c) Say no? Being a class president is too hard.

COACH REPROACH

2 After your last hockey game the coach approached you and asked you to pay more attention to your drop passes. Do you:
a) Tell him to take a hike? b) Spend the next week practicing the technique? c) Quit the hockey team?

AUDITION AMBITION

3 You really wanted to be the lead in the school play but they gave you the part of the servant instead. Do you:
a) Practice to be the best servant they've ever seen?
b) Sabotage the lead's lines during the show?
c) Not show up for rehearsal?

Interview Debut

4 Your first assignment for the school paper is to interview a local celebrity. Do you: a) Ask a friend to do it for you? b) Do some research and prepare your questions? c) Dread the interview so much that you plagiarize an article from the local newspaper?

Exam Jam

5 A big exam is coming up, and if you flunk this one you will fail the course! Do you: a) Study hard for weeks in advance? b) Call in sick the day of the exam? c) Devise a "one-cough-for-A, two-coughs-for-B" code with your friend?

UNCLEAR CHEER

6 You go to your sister's volleyball game. Do you: a) Make up a rude cheer insulting the opposing team's players? b) Spend the entire game at the snack bar? She'll probably lose anyway. c) Cheer her on and applaud the other team's good plays as well?

LOCKER ROOM DOOM

7 Your team has lost again to the Eagles. In the locker room, the team's frustration is so thick you could cut it with a knife. Do you: a) Admit you need more practice before the next game? b) Yell insults at the winning team? c) Drop out. You don't want to drag the team down.

DEBATE CHECKMATE

8 You ruled in the last debate! Your victory came as no surprise. Do you:
a) Snicker incessantly at the loser?
b) Congratulate your opponent and gracefully accept praise from audience members?
c) Act like it's no big deal.

Answers

1.	a) Game on b) Foul c) No show	2. a) Foul b) Game on c) No show	3 a) Game on b) Foul c) No show
4.	a) No show b) Game on c) Foul	5. a) Game on b) No show c) Foul	6. a) Foul b) No show c) Game on
7.	a) Game on b) Foul c) No show	8. a) Foul b) Game on c) No show	9. a) Game on b) No show c) Foul
10.	a) Foul b) No show c) Game on		

Hustle for Muscle

9 All the guys on your football team are really packing on the muscles. No matter what you do, you can't seem to keep up. Do you:
a) Keep working out and practicing?
b) Give up? c) Take a couple of steroid shots to boost your build?

A+ FUSS

10 Your A+ average is threatened when you are grouped with two B- students for a team project. Do you: a) Tell them you'll do everything and to simply write their names on the final copy? b) Try to ditch them and join another group? c) Share the workload and offer to help your teammates?

The **Underdog**

Let's face it — competition is not always what it's cracked up to be!

Maybe competing with others makes you very nervous. Maybe you avoid it and hope that it will simply go away. Everybody feels that way sometimes. Unfortunately, since competition is around us every day, it's better to learn how to handle it in a healthy way than to run from it.

Too Cool for Rules
Some people avoid competition by saying that they are "too cool" for the game, or that some things are "too stupid" to waste their time on. It's all right to not want to compete in certain activities, but it's never cool to ridicule something that someone else has worked hard to accomplish.

Have Realistic Goals
If you plan on being a millionaire by the time you're 15, chances are you will fail miserably. With more realistic goals — like having your own small summer business — your chances of succeeding will be better, and small setbacks won't throw you for a loop.

Visualize
Visualization is a technique that is used by many top athletes. You visualize, or imagine, yourself doing well in an upcoming event, like a test or a sports match. The point is to boost your confidence by having positive thoughts. Don't imagine everything could go wrong; picture all that will go right.

Keep Your Cool
Studying or practicing hard will help you feel more comfortable before and during a competition. If you don't know how to handle a problem right away, keep your cool and move on to the next one. The answer to your first problem could come to you while you're working ahead.

DID YOU KNOW?

- The best kind of success occurs when a person feels they have changed for the better by striving to reach their goals.

When Popularity Is Involved

Competition is pretty straightforward when it comes to sports or to academic performance — you win or you lose, you get an A or you don't. Things get a bit murkier is when popularity is involved. Who gets to sit at the "cool" table in the cafeteria? Who goes out with whom? In school, the drive to be popular often becomes really intense. If it's any comfort, know that the kids who are the most unpopular in your school right now probably won't be shunned once they get out into the "real world."

Of course, being popular has many advantages, including a secure group of friends with the same interests. But popularity is not as rosy as it seems from the outside. Somebody may try to take your place in the group, envious enough to try to oust you. Competing for popularity is a very slippery slope, especially when it starts to dictate all your other decisions. Just as being unpopular can weigh on your shoulders, the burdens that come with jockeying to stay on top can sometimes be too much to handle.

Here are a few examples of when competing to be popular has gone too far:
- **Consumer competition** — buying all the latest gizmos to "buy" others' approval.
- **Sexual competition** — bragging about the number of girlfriends or boyfriends you've had and how far you went with them to impress others.
- **Dangerous competition** — engaging in risky activities (drinking alcohol, taking drugs, fighting, etc.) to gain popularity.
- **Group competition** — joining a clique or gang simply to be seen with the "right" people, regardless of whether you like them or have the same interests; doing things that you know are wrong (stealing, skipping school, smoking, bullying others, etc.) to gain their approval.

For more about dealing with what others demand of you in the name of popularity, check out *Peer Pressure: Deal with it without losing your cool*, another book in the Deal With It series. Remember, if your health, your grades, or your self-esteem are being threatened by your need to be popular, you have a problem. It's better to be lonely for a while than to hurt yourself.

Send Up a Red Flag
If the pressure to compete becomes unbearable, it's important tell a trusted adult or friend. Surprisingly, most people will ease up when they know that they are pushing too hard.

- Teamwork is a great way to learn how to support and cooperate with others and to enjoy each other's successes.

- Some people think our "animal instincts" drive us to compete. In fact, many species live in packs, and work together to survive.

The **Spectator**

Do you have a sister who cries every time she loses? Know someone who cheats? Have a friend who struggles with school marks?

If you've noticed that people around you are having a hard time dealing with the pressures of competition, there are things you can do to help them.

It's sometimes hard to understand how people can react so differently to the same situation, especially if you've never felt that way yourself. A pop quiz in your science class could simply be a groaner for you, but for the kid at the next desk it could trigger stomach pains and cold sweats. A 3 to 0 score in your badminton match could mean disappointment to you, but a crushing defeat to your teammate. Sometimes, what we do and say can actually make things worse for a person who's struggling.

By paying attention to how different people react to competition, you also have the power to help them handle it in a healthier way!

Ease Up!

Cheating, mouthing off, crying, and arrogance are all signs that someone's need to win has gotten out of control. If you know someone who acts this way, you can help by:

- keeping your calm, even when things get heated.

- comforting the person who takes losing to heart by letting them know that you are still a friend, no matter if they win or lose.

- being a good example — always congratulate winners and be sympathetic to the losing team, accept the outcome of the game without complaints or excuses, and play by the rules.

- letting cheaters and gloaters know that you don't agree with what they are doing.

Under Your Wing

Some kids have a very hard time dealing with the thought of losing, and so they avoid competition. If you know anyone who tends to shy away, gets very nervous, or even becomes sick at the thought of any type of confrontation, you can help boost their confidence by:

- reminding them of times when things have gone right.

- helping them practice or study before a test.

- trying to have fun while competing.

- reminding them that you will still be friends whether they win or lose.

do's and don'ts

✓ Do tell cheaters how their actions make you feel, if you feel it is safe to do so.

✓ Do anonymously report cheaters to a sympathetic adult like a teacher, a parent, or a counsellor.

✓ Do offer your support to kids who are struggling with the pressures of competition.

✓ If someone's health is at risk, do let that person know you are concerned and get help.

✓ Do suggest cooperative activities instead of always playing competitive games.

✓ Do let your buddies know that you will be their friend no matter the outcome of a test or a game.

✓ Do ask how something went and if a competitor had fun, instead of always focusing on who won.

✓ Do set a good example by being a good sport.

✗ Don't join in when teammates are bad-mouthing other teams, coaches, or referees.

✗ Don't chant along with humiliating or degrading cheers.

✗ Don't call people losers.

✗ Don't judge someone's worth by their grades or how they do in sports.

✗ Don't get caught up in the actions of poor sports.

✗ Don't cheat, even when you are up against a cheater.

27

The **Spectator**

QUIZ

Do you really get it?

Okay, so you think that you know what to do if you see someone being too competitive. But do you really get it? What would you do in the following situations? This quiz has no right or wrong answers, because each situation is unique. Your answers may be different from the ones given below, but they could be right under the circumstances.

PARENT PRESSURE

(2) You have a friend whose parents are never happy with the marks that he brings home, and are giving him a really hard time about his grades in a particular class. Now your friend does nothing but study. He barely sleeps anymore!

Mean Martial Arts

(1) A guy in your tae kwon do class always hurts others on purpose. When he loses, he gets really ticked off and makes sure that he hurts his opponent in the next match.

- Tell the coach you have concerns. He or she may talk to your teammate about his aggressive behaviour.
- Hold a team meeting, discussing how the team wants to compete.
- Report your teammate's actions to an official of your sport who can stop your friend from purposely hurting anyone else in the match.

ST. IGNATIUS HIGH SCHOOL

- If you study with your friend, be encouraging about how well he knows the material.
- Let your friend know that you are worried about his health and the way he is handling the pressure his parents are putting on him.
- Encourage your friend to talk to a teacher, a counsellor, or the principal of your school. They may be able to let your friends' parents know how well your friend is doing and to tell them that they need not be concerned with a few bad test results.

Cheat Trick

(3) Your best friend cheats in class and gets away with it. She has better grades than you do and she's not even studying!

- Tell your friend how her cheating makes you feel. If she sees that what she is doing hurts you, she may change her ways.
- Talk about your concern to the teacher, without mentioning any names.
- If your friend won't respect your feelings about cheating, consider spending more time with people who are not so competitive.

CHECK MATES

(4) Over the summer, you discover that you have a talent for playing chess. Your friends think that chess is for losers and nerds. You want to join the chess club, but are afraid that they will make fun of you.

- Explain to your friends that chess is similar to the strategy games they play on their game systems or computers.
- Remind your friends that different people are good at different things.
- Join the chess club, and remember that your true friends will support you.

Who Cares?

(5) Your brother acts like he doesn't care about school. He's always showing up late, not handing in his assignments, and doodling on his books. You know he is really smart, and don't understand why he doesn't even try.

- When some people are under a lot of pressure to succeed, their fear of failure can be very painful. Ask your brother whether his attitude is covering up a bigger worry about his schoolwork.
- Encourage your brother to talk to your parents about it.
- Suggest studying together, which he might find less stressful than going it alone.
- Talk to a teacher or counsellor about your concerns. If they know why he goofs off, they might have ideas for helping him do better.

Continues ...

STICKY FINGERS

6 The kids at your school are always trying to have the coolest gadgets. You are in an electronics store and you see a girl from your class shoplifting a handheld data organizer.

- Let her know that you have seen what she is doing. Tell her you will tell store security if she doesn't put it back on the display.
- Ask your friends why it is important to have the latest thing and whether the competition can ever be won.
- Talk to a counsellor about your concerns, without mentioning any names.

Bumping the Ump

8 In gym class, you have been assigned umpire duty in a baseball game. When you rule a player out, she screams and pushes you, saying you are biased because your best friend is on the other team. Members of both teams start getting angry.

- Ask her to calm down or she will be out of the game.
- Call a time-out. Tell both teams that everyone has to cool it if the game is going to continue.
- Ask a coach or the phys. ed. teacher to intervene.

Bored of Board Games

7 When your best friend wins, he gloats in front of everyone else. When you beat him, he accuses you of cheating and tells people you can't be trusted.

- Tell him that his competitive streak makes you uncomfortable.
- Ask him to stop spreading rumours that affect your reputation even if he is joking. Other people won't know he isn't being serious.
- Try to find cooperative games to play together.

DID YOU KNOW?

- By age 9, kids start judging and competing with friends for the best clothes, gadgets, and other possessions.

'Roid Rage

9 You find out that your friend has been spending all his time at the gym so he can lose weight. Instead of looking healthier, he seems tired and doesn't eat much.

- Ask your friend why he is driving himself so hard.
- Suggest other less intense ways he can stay fit, like joining a team sport or walking.
- If your friend's health is in danger, tell him you are concerned and get help from a trusted adult.

DOUBLES TROUBLE

10 You are playing doubles tennis against really skilled players. At first, your partner goes after every shot, not letting you play. Then she says she is forfeiting the game because of her injured foot. The thing is, her foot looks fine, and you know she just doesn't want to lose.

- Tell her that if she lets you play, then the loss won't be hers alone, but will be shared between you.
- Tell her that even though you are losing you would like to get in some practice.
- Ask her to finish "for fun," without the results being posted.
- Ask your opponents if one of them can sit out the rest of the game so at least two of you can keep playing. Maybe your partner will see how silly she is being.

- Over 25 million children throughout Canada and the US participate in some form of organized sports.

- In a study, young athletes were asked why they play sports. "To have fun" was the top reason given. "Winning" ranked 10th.

More Help

It takes time and practice to learn the skills in this book. There are many ways to deal with competition, but only you know which feels right in each situation. In the end, the best response is the one that keeps you safe.

If you need more help, or someone to talk to, the following resources may be of help.

Helplines

Kids Help Phone (Canada)   1-800-668-6868
Youth Crisis Hotline (USA)   1-800-448-4663

Web sites

AADAC Youth Services: www.Zoot2.com

Deal.org

Go All the Way… Without Drugs: www.rcmp-grc.gc.ca/das/go_all_way_e.htm

Health Canada – Just for You (Youth) http://www.hc-sc.gc.ca/english/for_you/youth.html

Kids Help Phone: http://kidshelp.sympatico.ca

National Eating Disorders Centre: www.nedic.ca

Rage Against Roids: www.hc-sc.gc.ca/hppb/hiv_aids/youth/roids/

Red Cross Interactive Info for Youth: www.redcross.ca

Schoolnet.ca

Youthpath.ca

Books

Brothers on Ice by John Danakas. James Lorimer & Company, 2001.

Crossing the Line by A. D. Fast. Vanwell Publishing, 2003.

Dangerous Rivals by A.D. Fast. Vanwell Publishing, 2002.

Dealing With Competitiveness by Don Middleton. Power Kids Press, 1999.

Good Sports: Winning, Losing, and Everything in Between by Therese Kauchak. Pleasant Company Publications, 1999.

Just for Kicks by Robert Rayner. James Lorimer & Company, 2004.

Making the Grade by H.G. Sotzek. Vanwell, 2003.

Miss Little's Losers by Robert Rayner. James Lorimer & Company, 2003.

Muscle Bound by H.A. Levigne. Vanwell Publishing, 2002.

Off Track by Bill Swan. James Lorimer & Company, 2003.

Play Ball by Carol Matas. Key Porter Books, 2004.

Road Trip by Eric Walters. Orca Book Publishers, 2002.

Roid Rage by Lesley Choyce. Harbour Publishing, 1999.

Spitfire by Ann Goldring. Raincoast Books, 2001.

A Stroke of Luck by Kathryn Ellis. James Lorimer & Company, 1995.

Tag Team by Paul Kropp. Hi Interest Publishing, 2002.

Teenage Competition – A Survival Guide by Susan and Daniel Cohen. M. Evans & Company Inc., 1986.

Water Fight by Michele Martin Bossley. James Lorimer & Company, 1996.

Winning and Losing by Lowell A. Dickmeyer & Martha Humphreys. Easy-Read Sports Book, 1984.

Text copyright © 2004 by Mireille Messier
Illustrations copyright © 2004 by Steven Murray

James Lorimer & Company Ltd. acknowledges the support of the Ontario Arts Council. We acknowledge the support of the Government of Canada through the Book Publishing Industry Development Program (BPIDP) for our publishing activities. We acknowledge the support of the Canada Council for the Arts for our publishing program. We acknowledge the support of the Government of Ontario through the Ontario Media Development Corporation's Ontario Book Initiative.

The Canada Council | Le Conseil des Arts
for the Arts | du Canada

ONTARIO ARTS COUNCIL
CONSEIL DES ARTS DE L'ONTARIO

Design: Blair Kerrigan/Glyphics

National Library of Canada Cataloguing in Publication Data

Messier, Mireille, 1971-

   Competition : deal with it from start to finish / Mireille Messier.

Includes bibliographical references.

ISBN 1-55028-832-6

   1. Competition (Psychology) in children— Juvenile literature. I. Title.

BF723.C6M47 2004   j302'.14   C2004-900478-6

James Lorimer & Company Ltd., Publishers
35 Britain Street
Toronto, Ontario
M5A 1R7
www. lorimer.ca

Distributed in the United States by:
Orca Book Publishers
P.O. Box 468 Custer, WA
USA 98240-0468

Printed and bound in China